The Elephant Who Wanted to Fly.

"The Importance of Dreaming and Accepting Who We Are""

2024

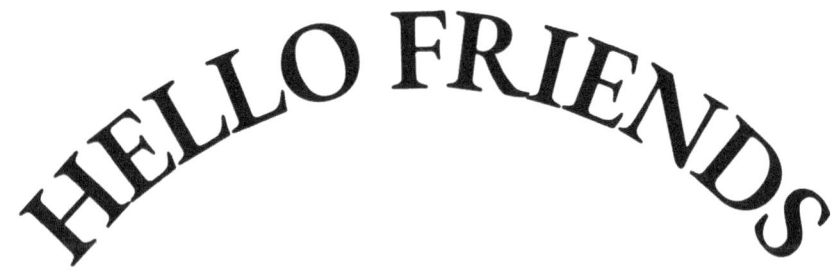

Welcome, dear little readers, to an incredible story that will take us to "The Elephant Who Wanted to Fly"!

Get ready for an incredible journey.

Tonico, an elephant full of dreams, wanted something that seemed impossible: to fly like the birds. With the help of his friends from the forest, he embarks on a fun adventure to try to make his wish come true. But along the way, Tonico discovers that the real magic is not in flying, but in accepting and valuing who he really is. A charming story about dreams, friendship and the beauty of being unique.

READY? LET'S START

Tonico was an elephant with a dreamy heart,

He lived looking at the sky with deep fervor.

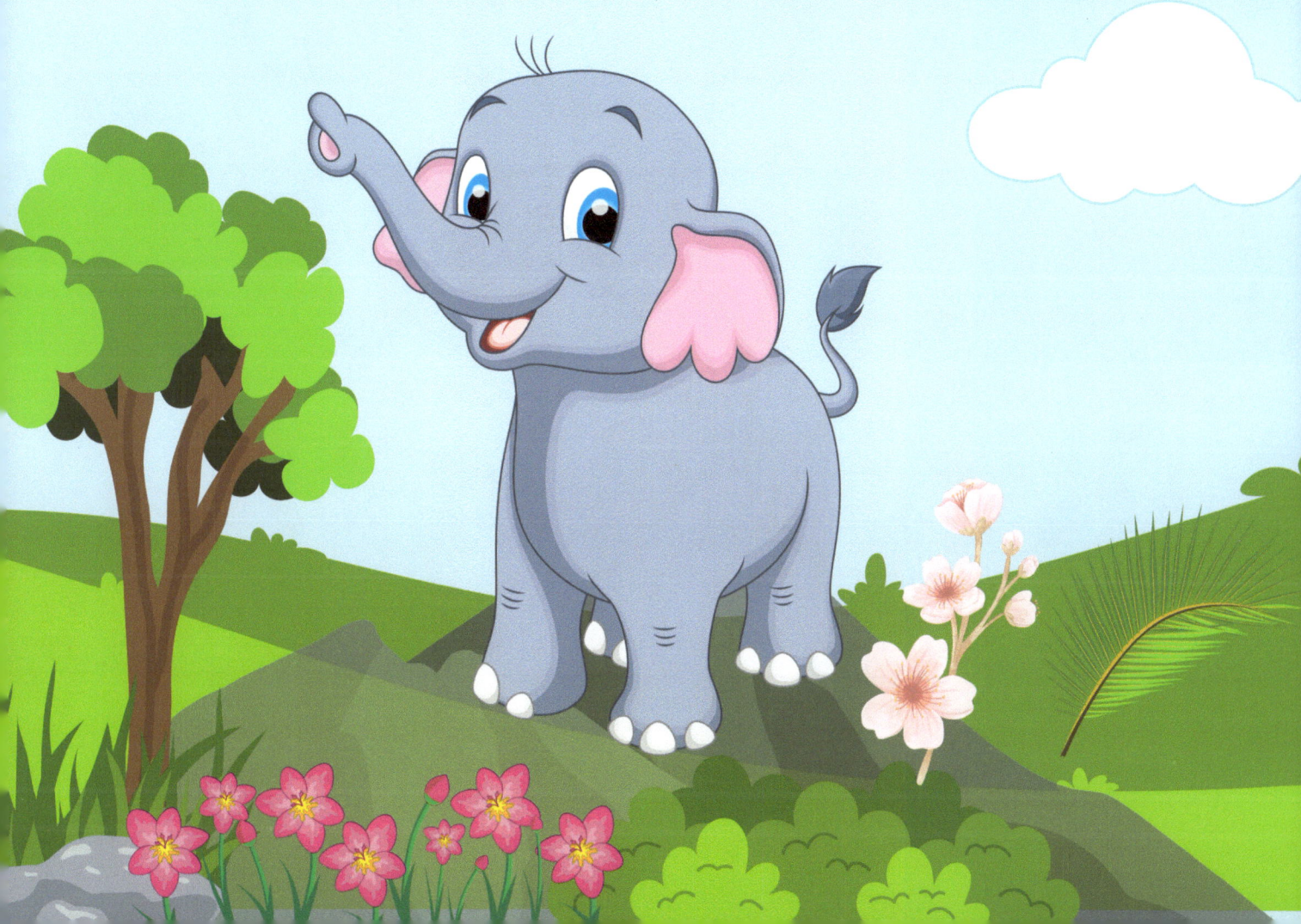

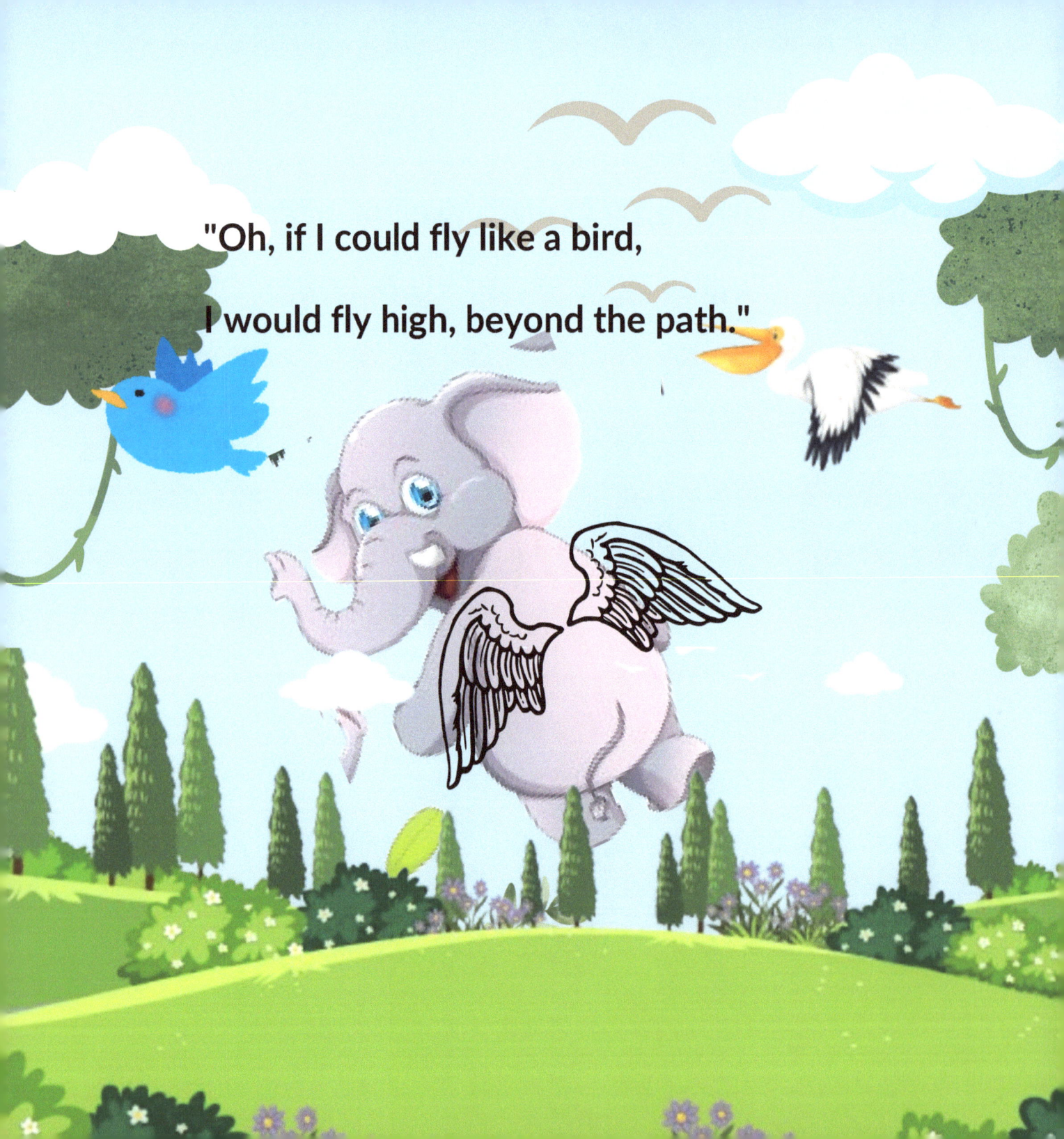

"Oh, if I could fly like a bird,

I would fly high, beyond the path."

The friends laughed, but explained affectionately,

"Elephants don't fly, they stay on the ground!"

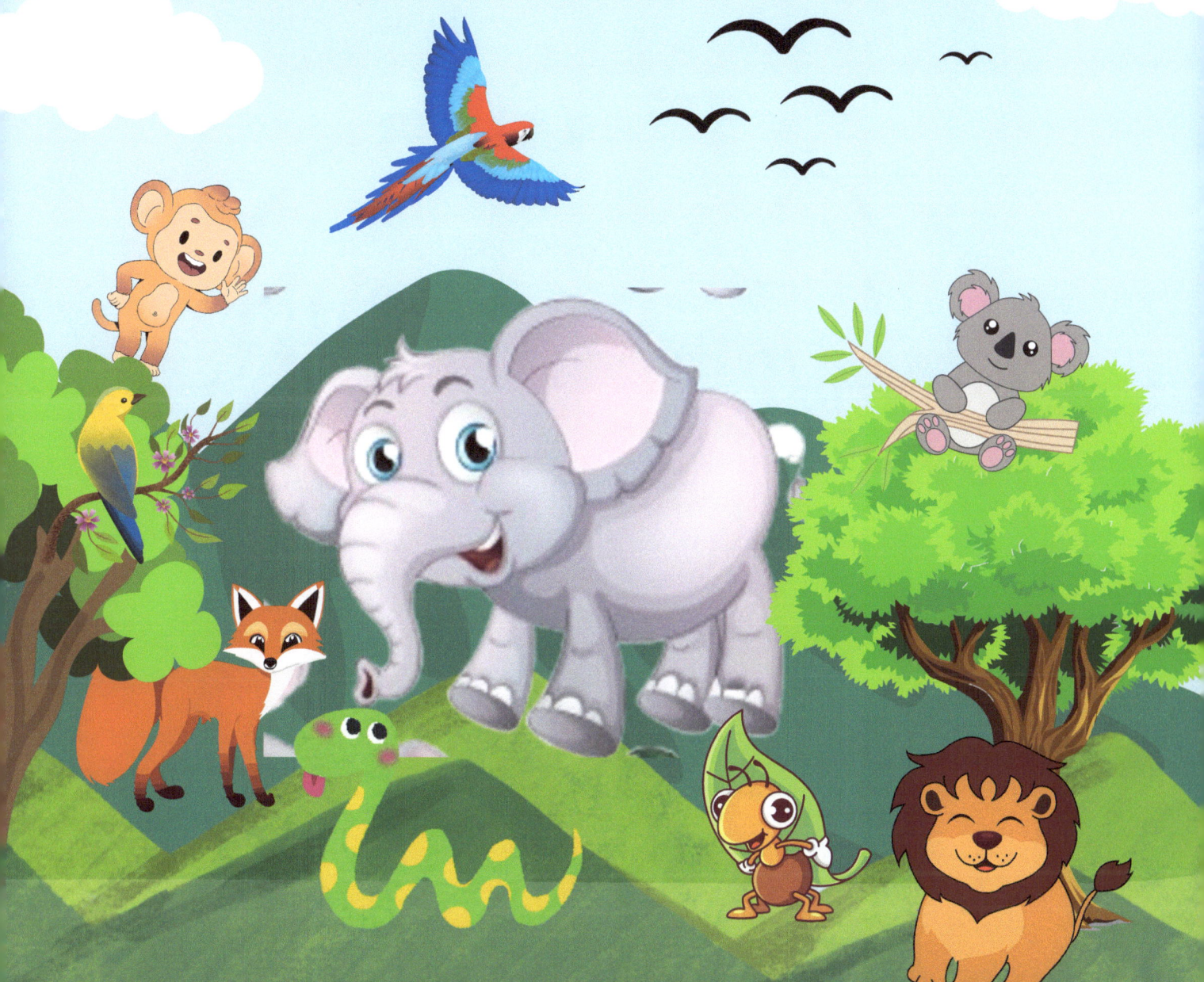

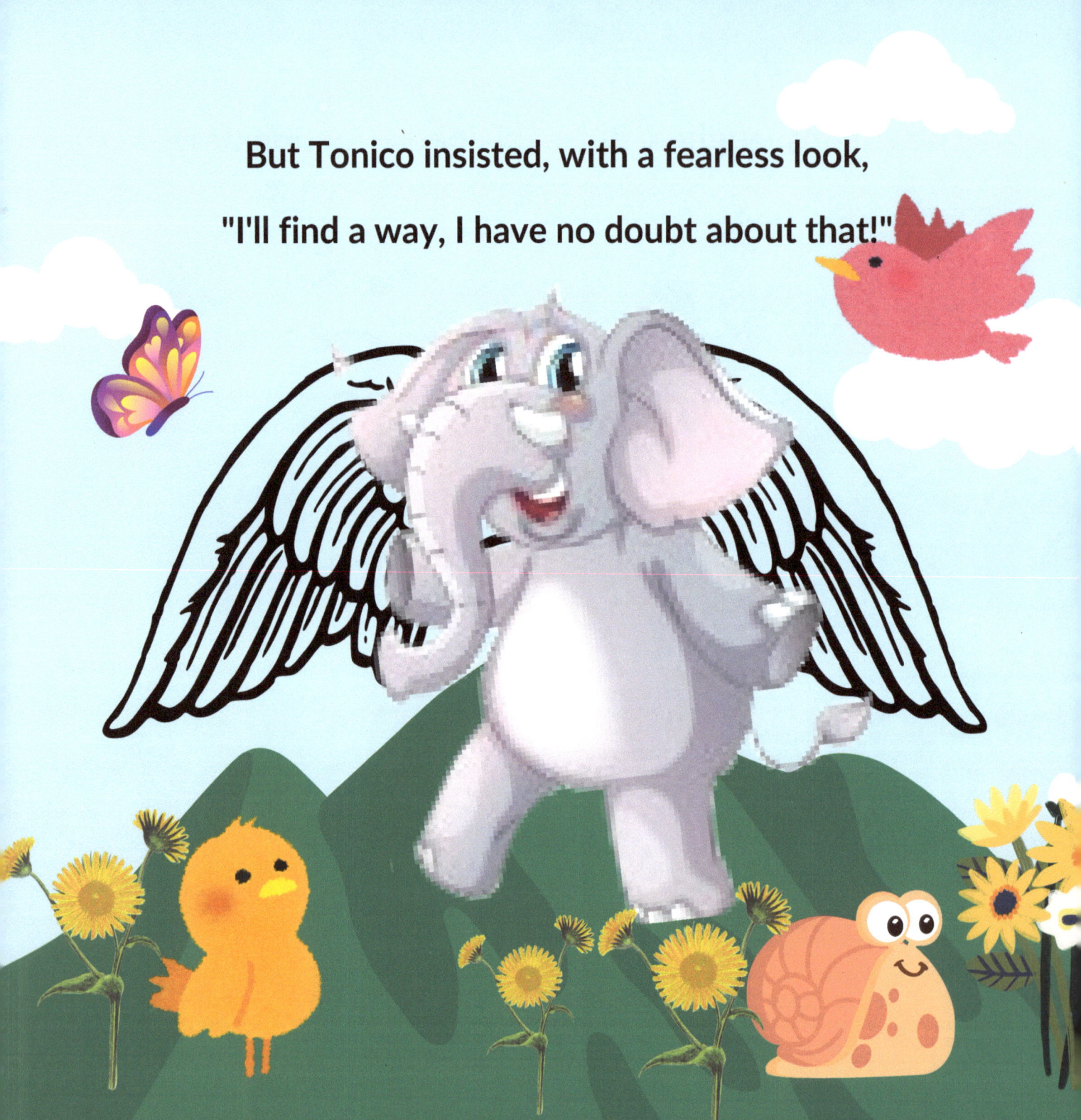

But Tonico insisted, with a fearless look,

"I'll find a way, I have no doubt about that!"

He tried to use leaves, he made them his wings,

He jumped from a rock, but fell into the embers.

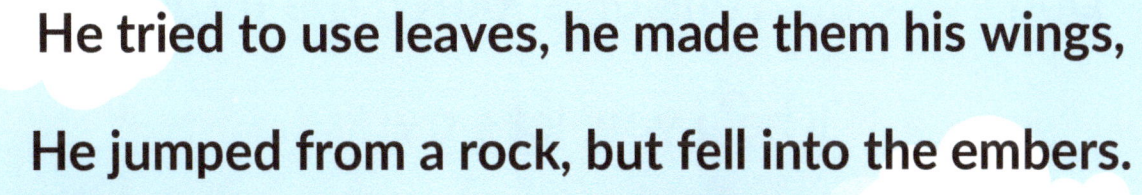

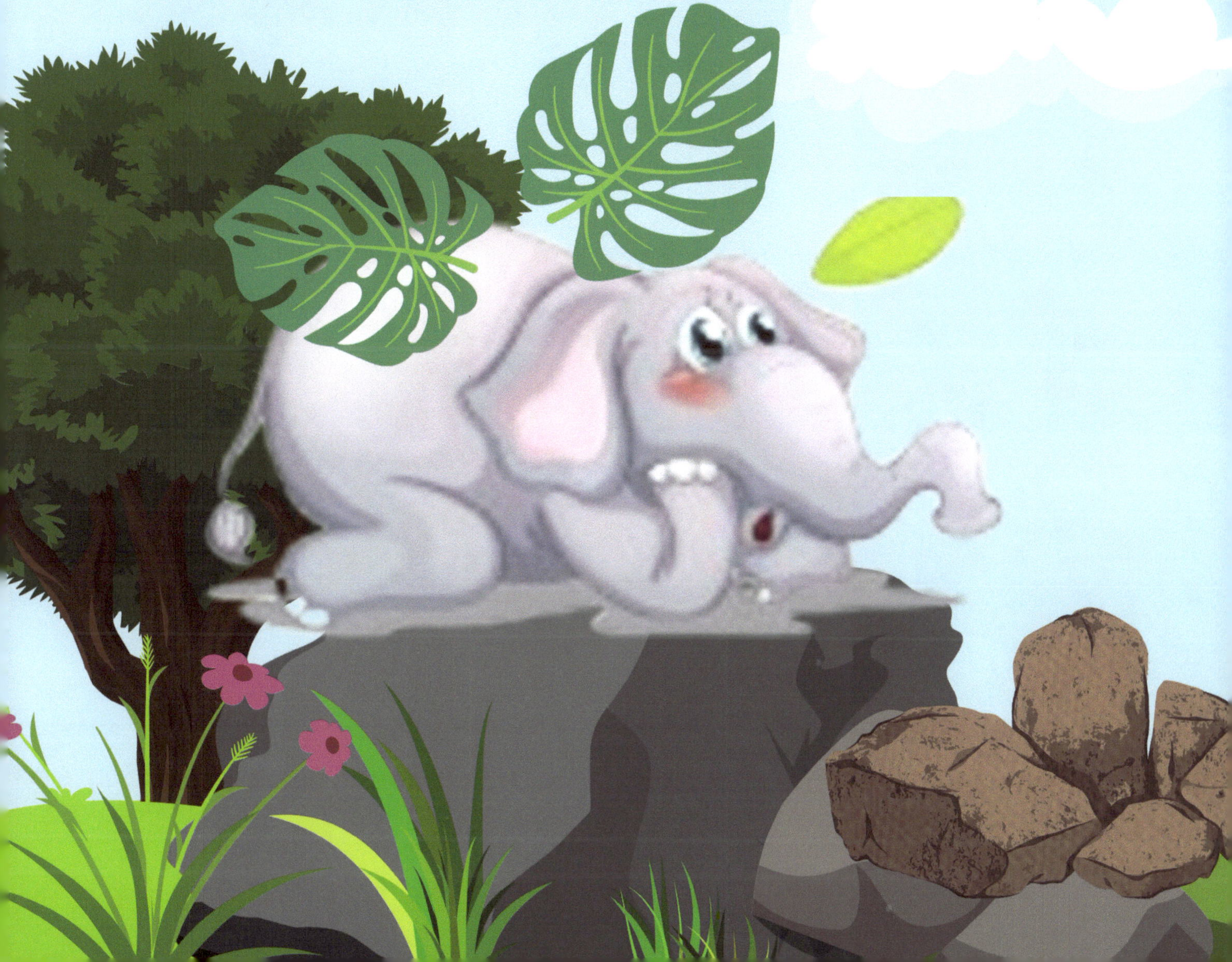

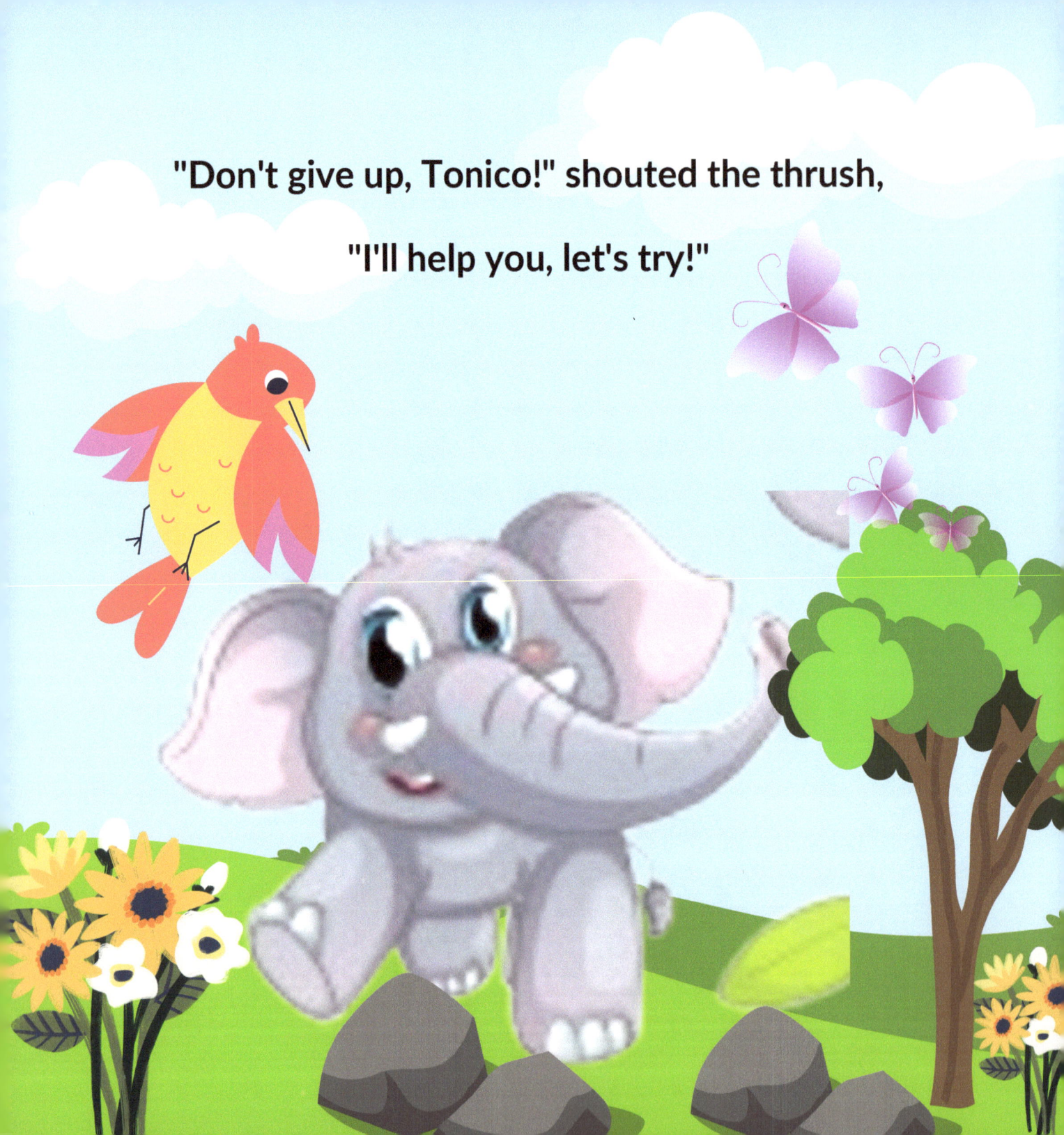

"Don't give up, Tonico!" shouted the thrush,

"I'll help you, let's try!"

They built a wing out of branches and leaves,

But the wind was strong, and everything fell apart.

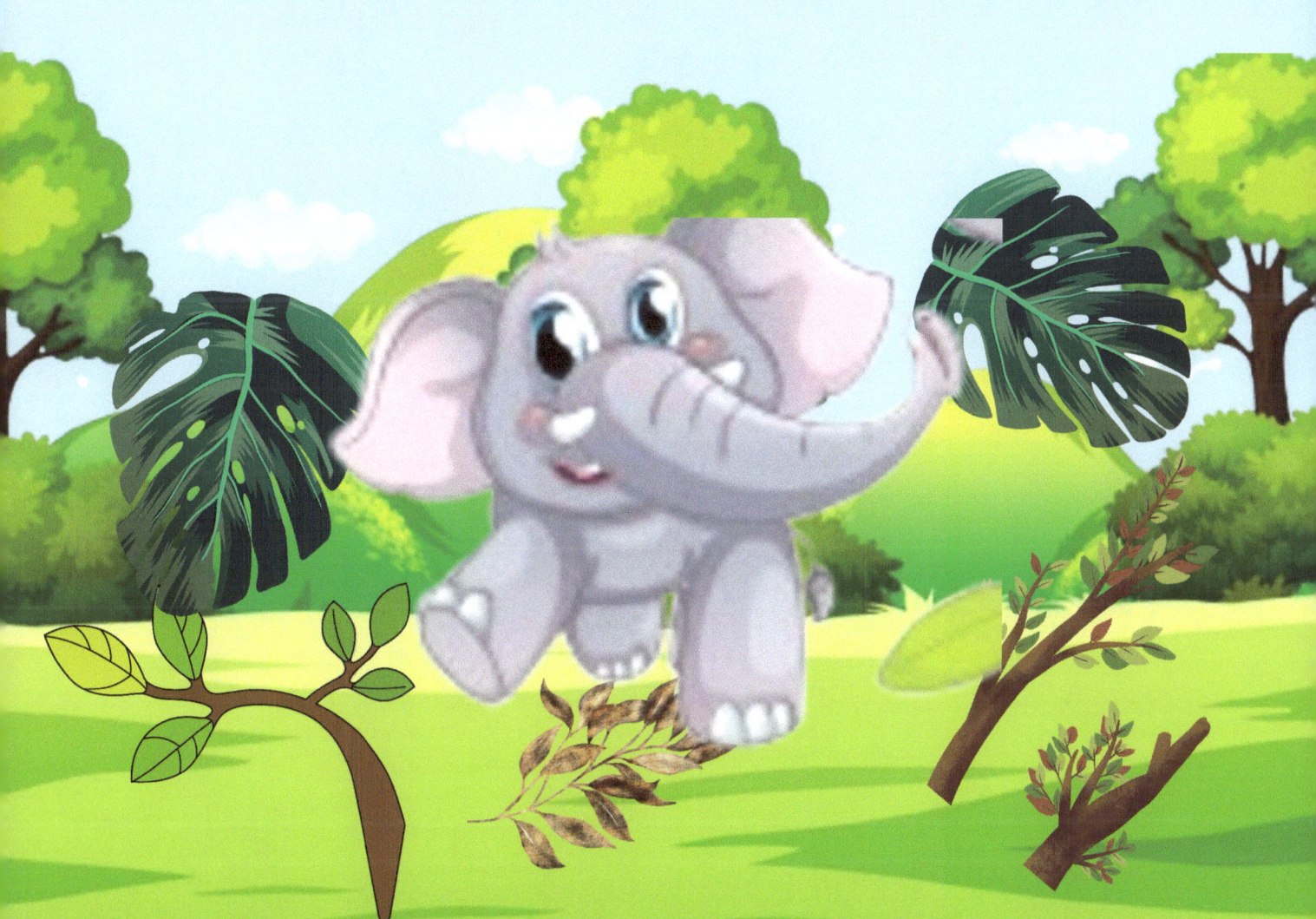

Even so, Tonico didn't stop trying,

Deep in his chest, the dream shines.

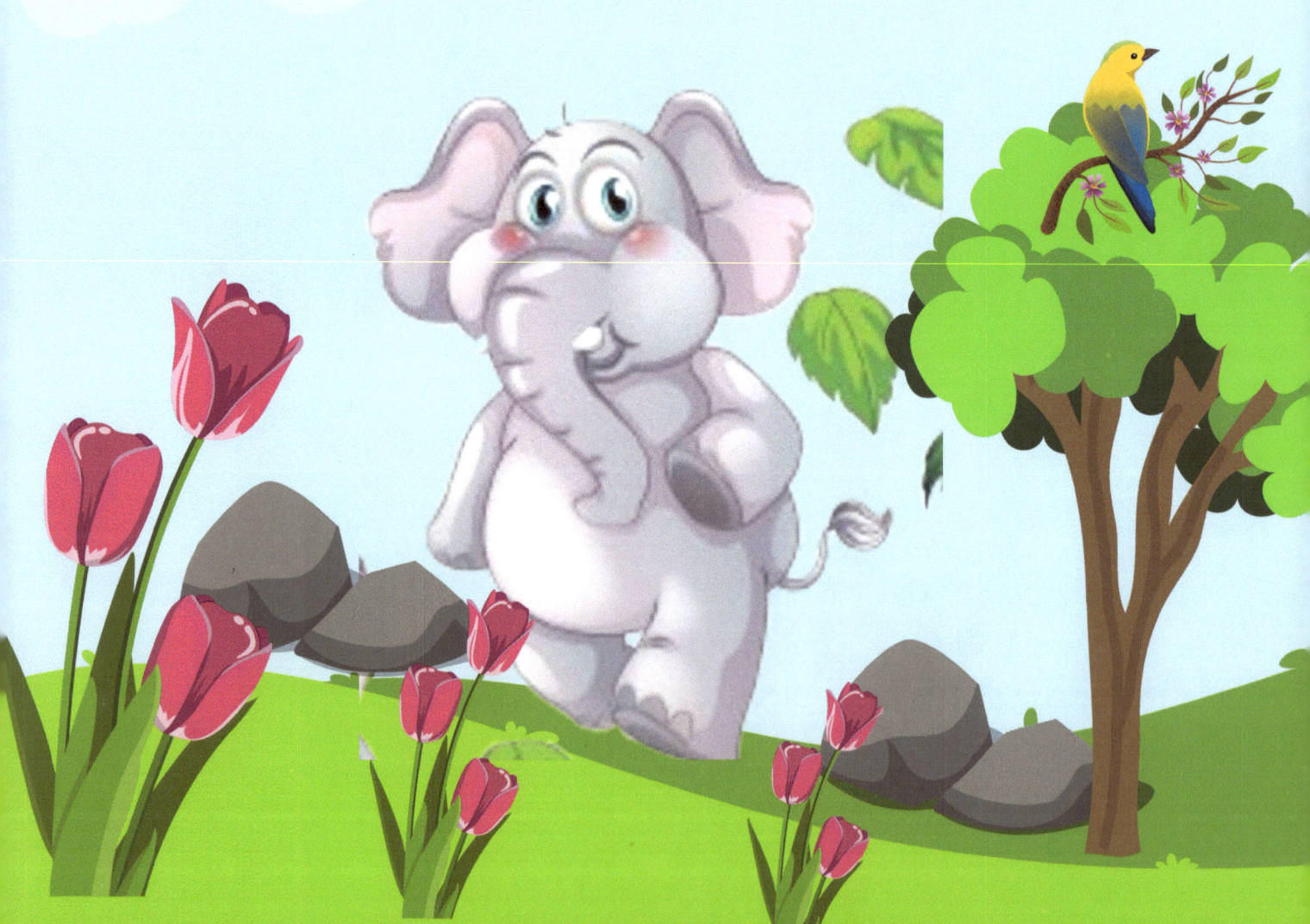

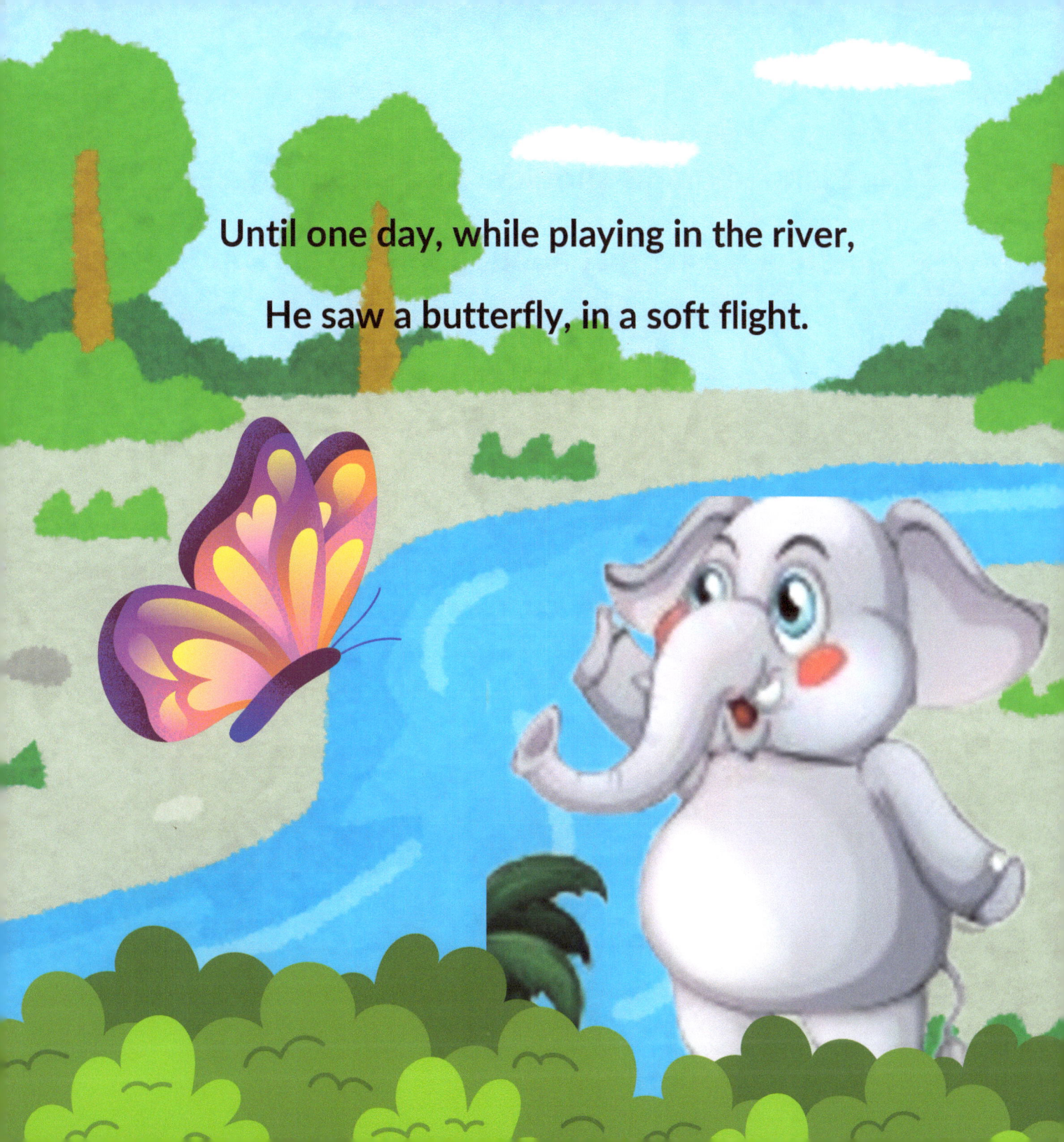
Until one day, while playing in the river,

He saw a butterfly, in a soft flight.

She landed on his shoulder and said with a smile,

"Flying isn't just about going up and up."

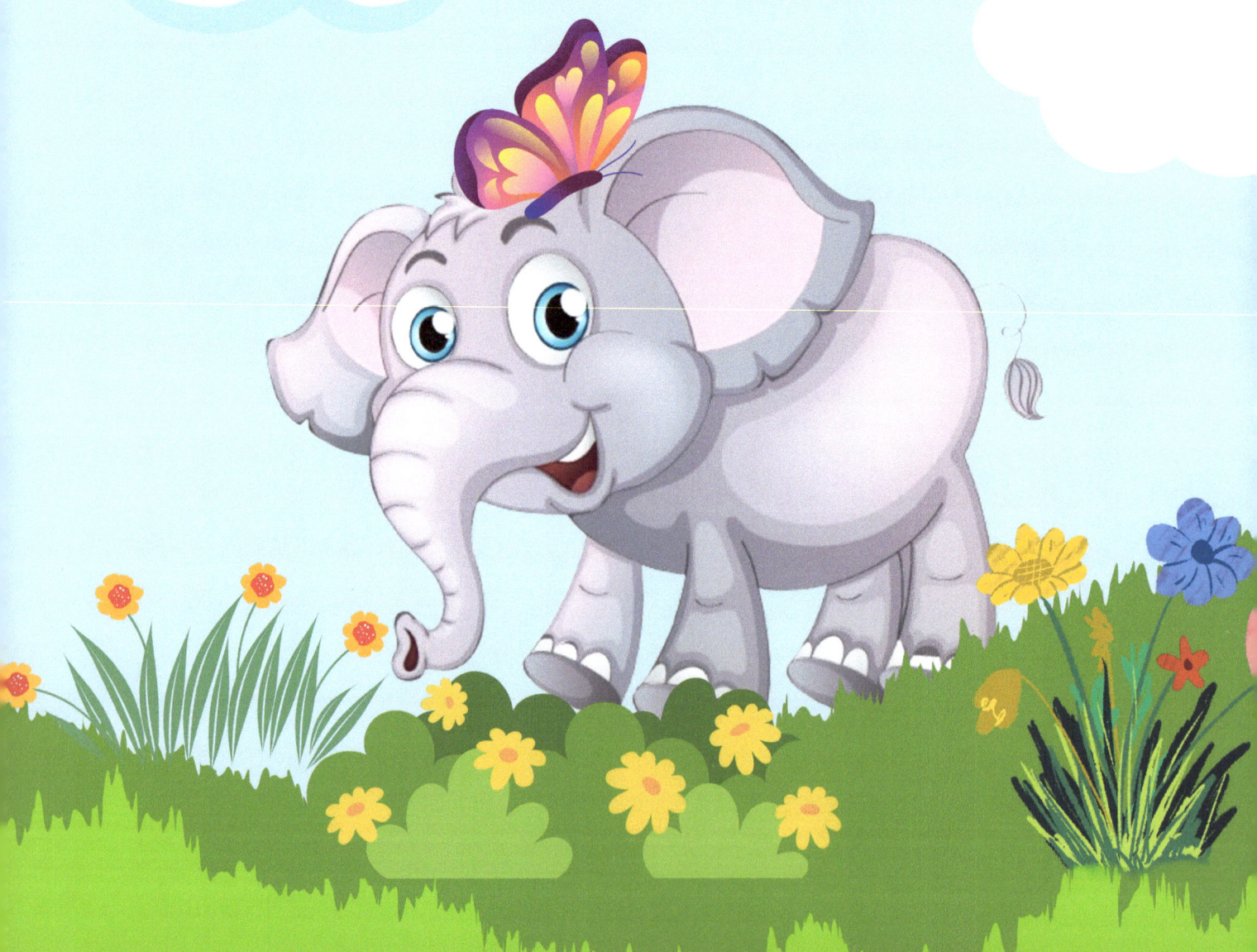

"You are special, you have strength and you have weight.

But you also have a heart, and that is what I value.

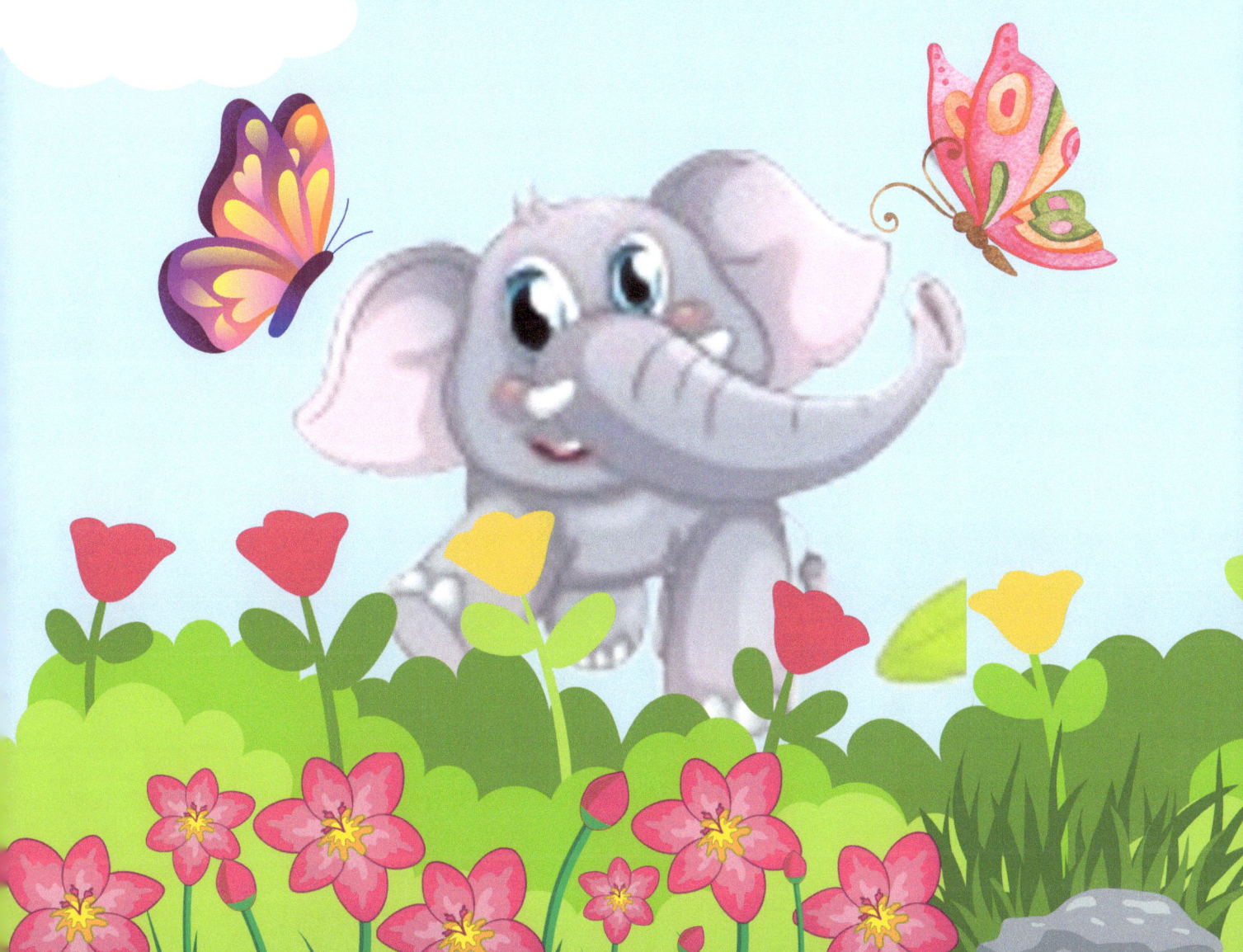

What matters is not the flight up in the air,

But the greatness of being who you are, without changing."

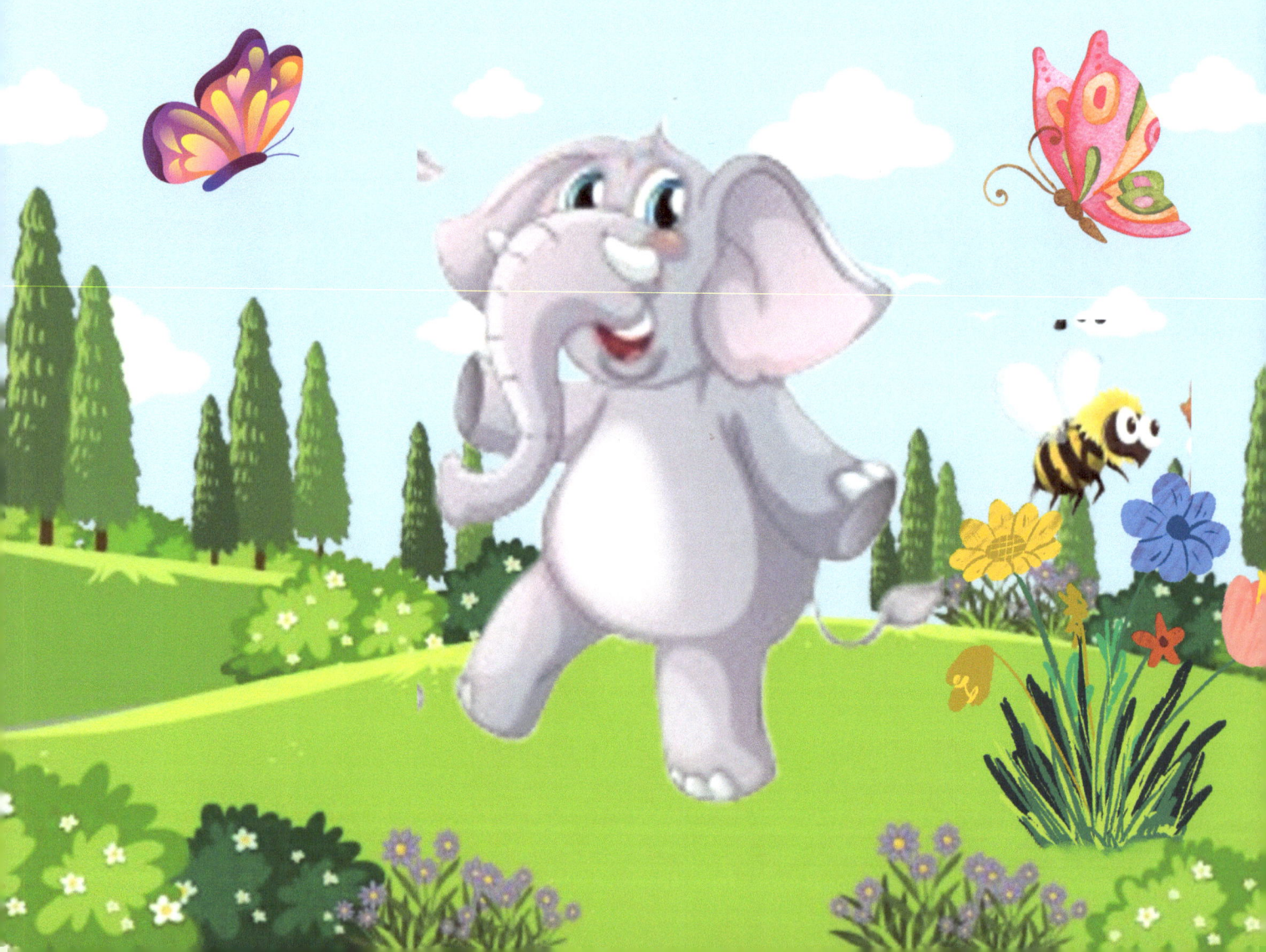

Tonico thought and, in an instant, he understood,

That he didn't need to fly to be who he is.

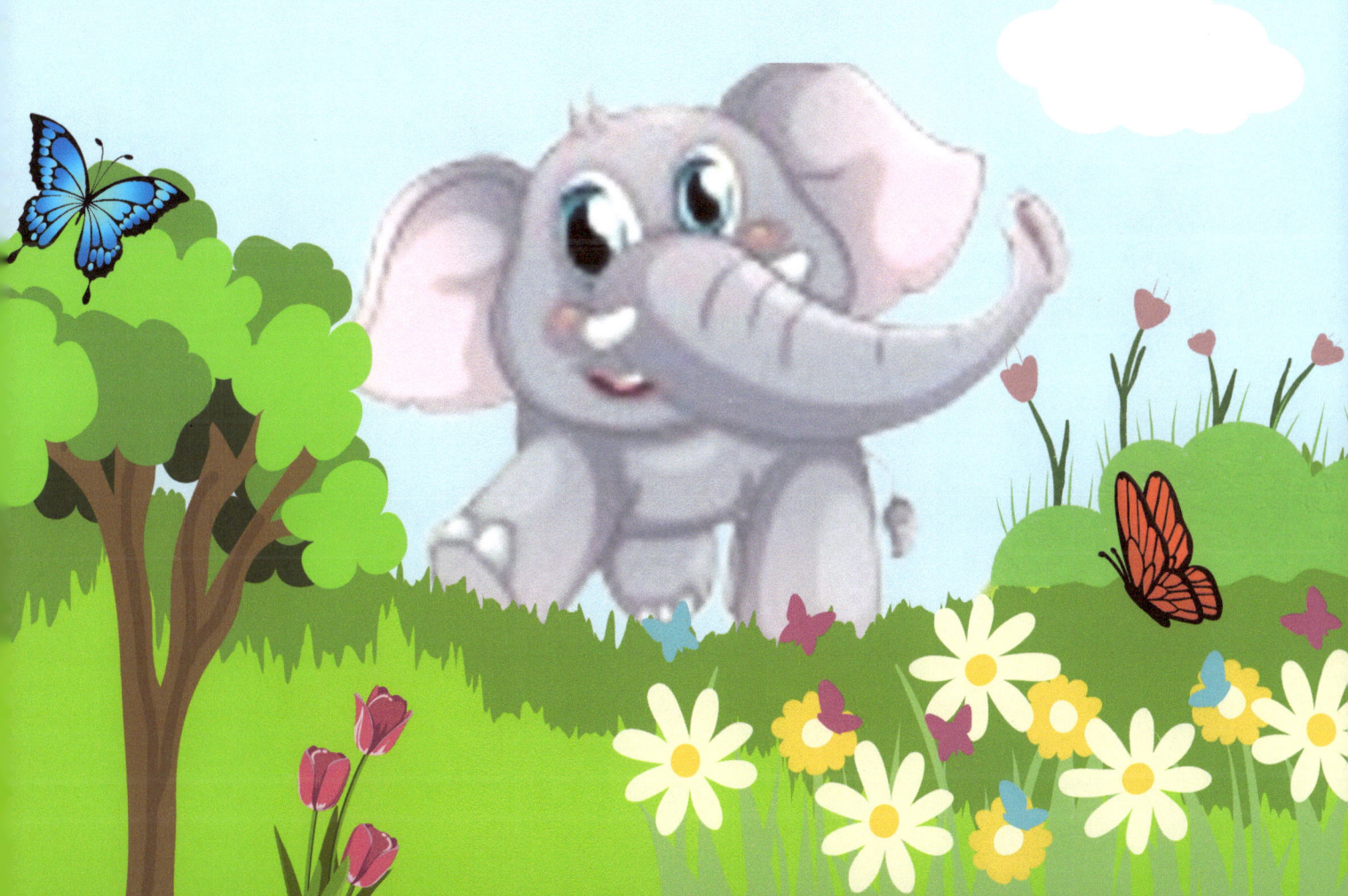

With his feet steady, he could explore,

The beauty of the world, without needing to fly.

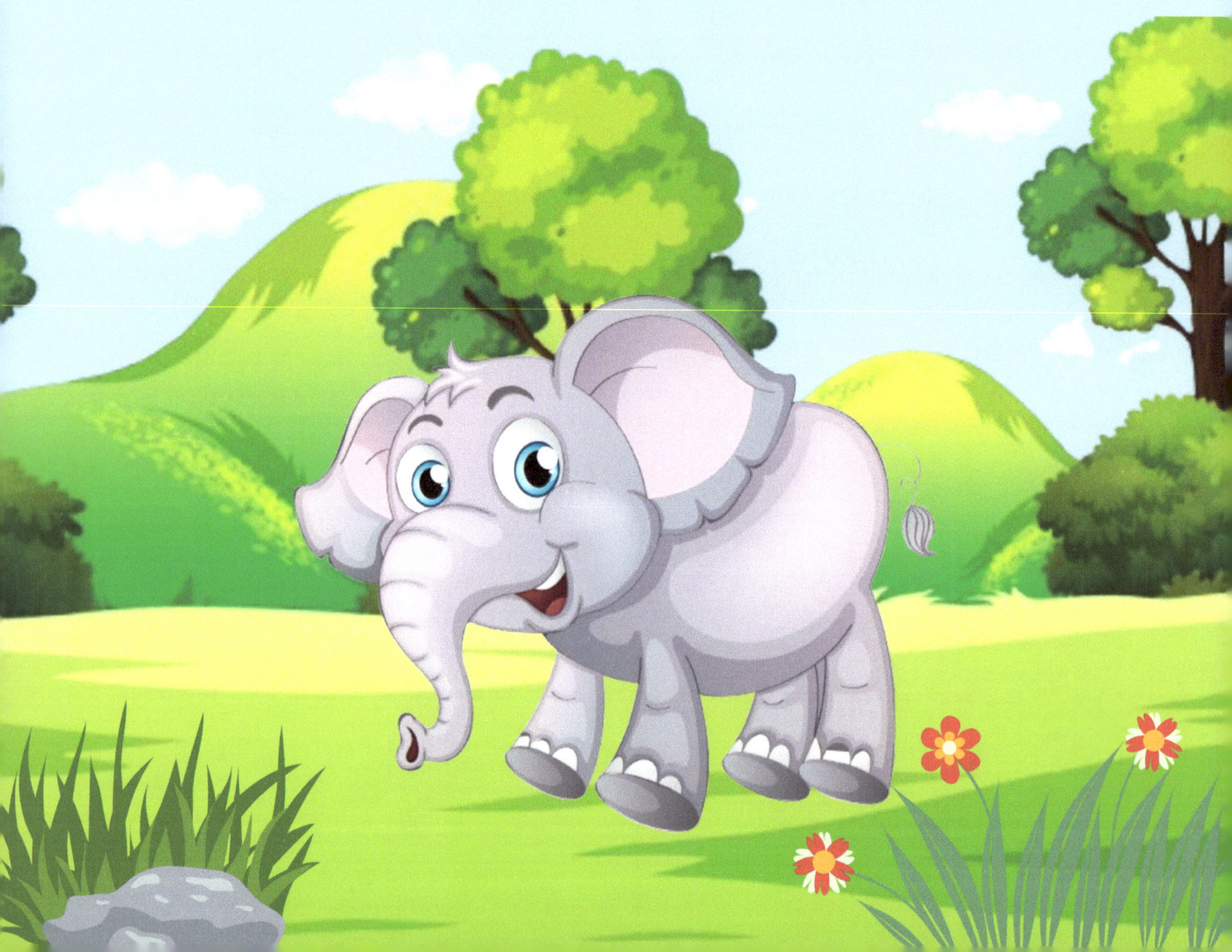

And so, he stopped trying to imitate,

And accepted his form, with pride in walking.

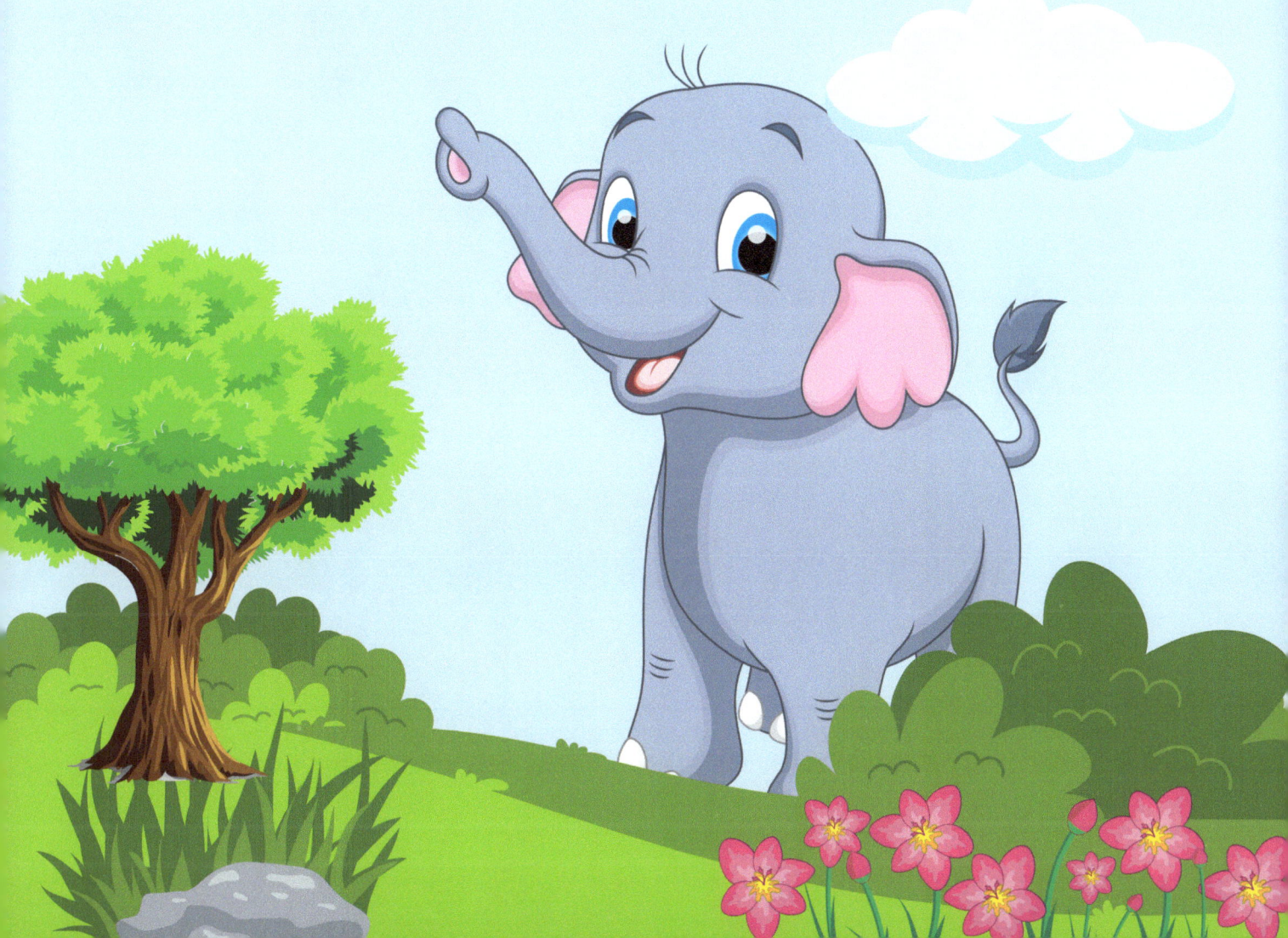

The friends applauded, full of emotion,

Because Tonico found his true lesson.

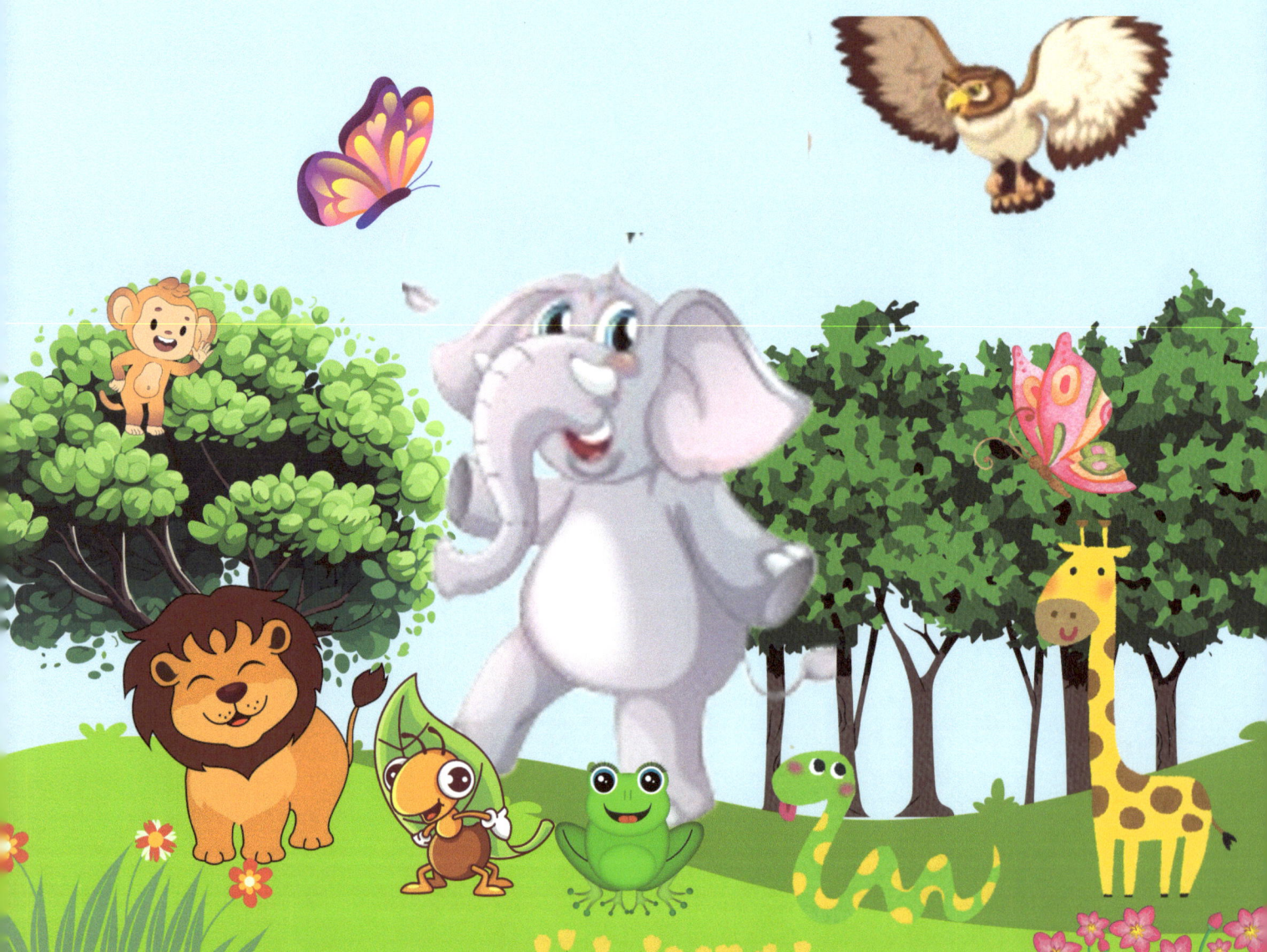

Now he dances, without fear of making mistakes,

He knows that strength lies in his way of loving.

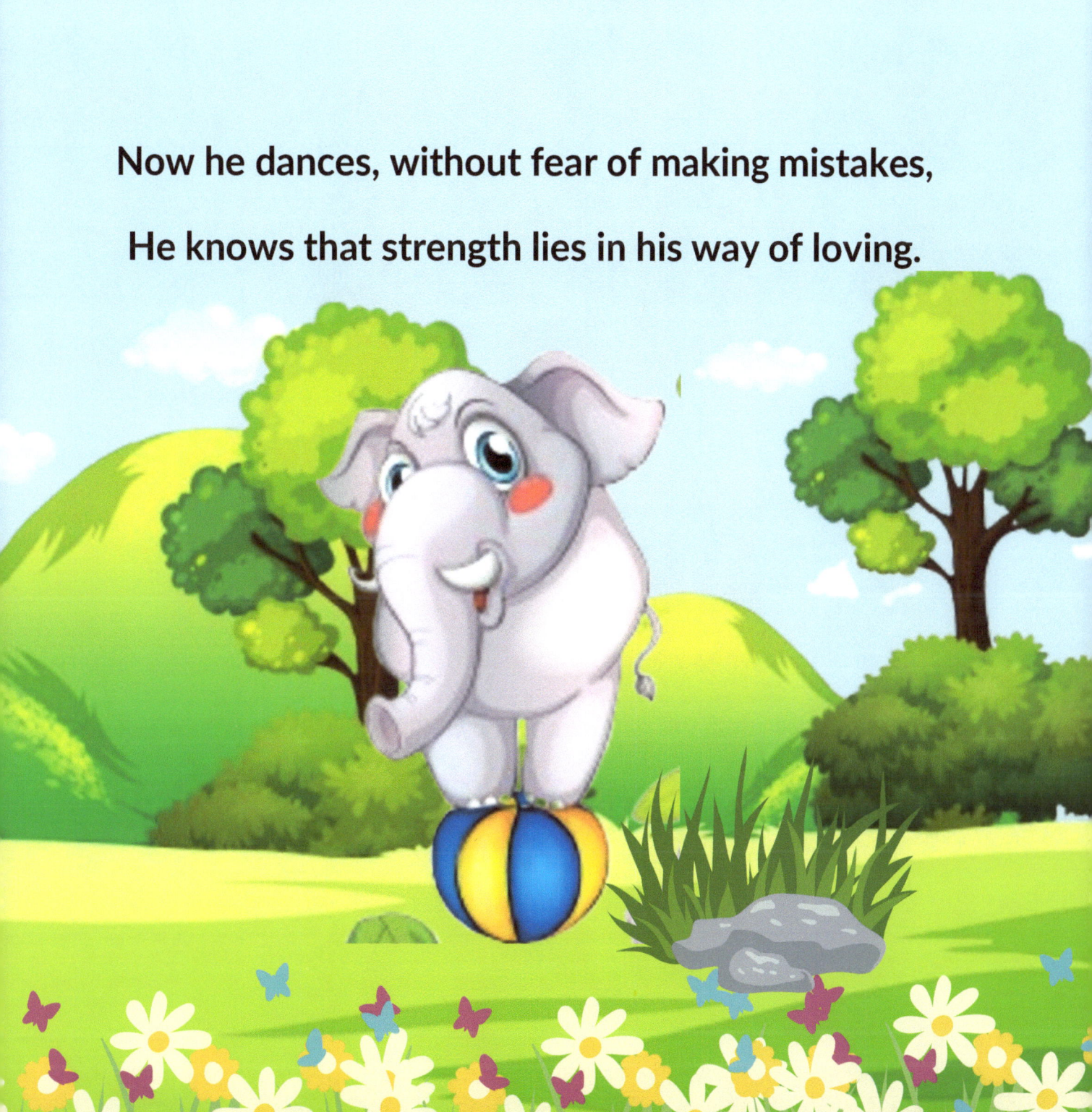

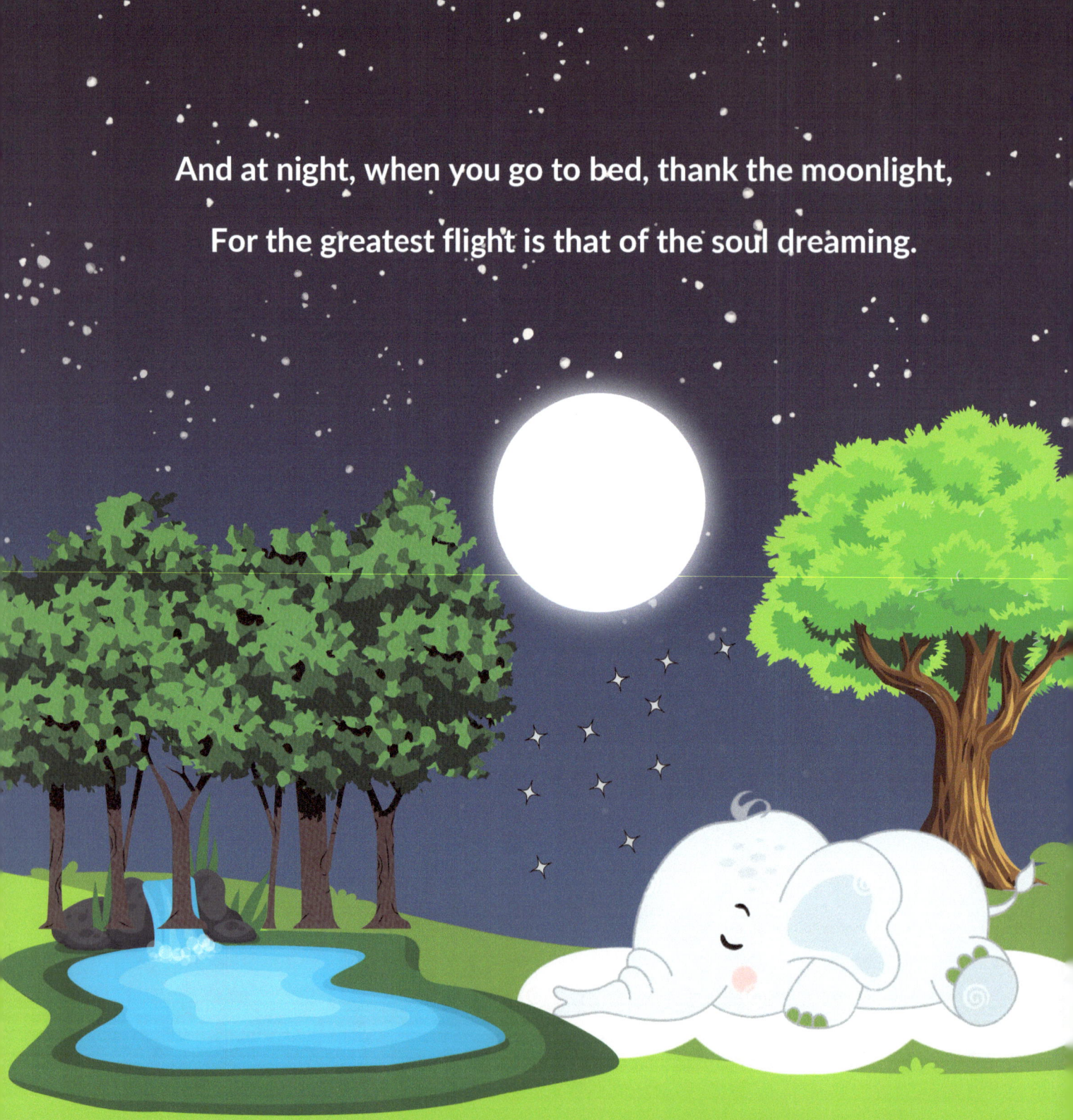

And at night, when you go to bed, thank the moonlight,

For the greatest flight is that of the soul dreaming.

Summary:

Tonico, the dreamy elephant, wanted to reach the sky and fly like the birds. On his journey, he tried everything, with the help of his friends, to make this wish come true. However, along the way, Tonico discovered that it was not necessary to fly to be special. By accepting who he was and appreciating his unique qualities, he learned a valuable lesson: true magic is within us, and dreams can take us to higher places than we imagine.

A story about dreams, acceptance and the power of friendship.

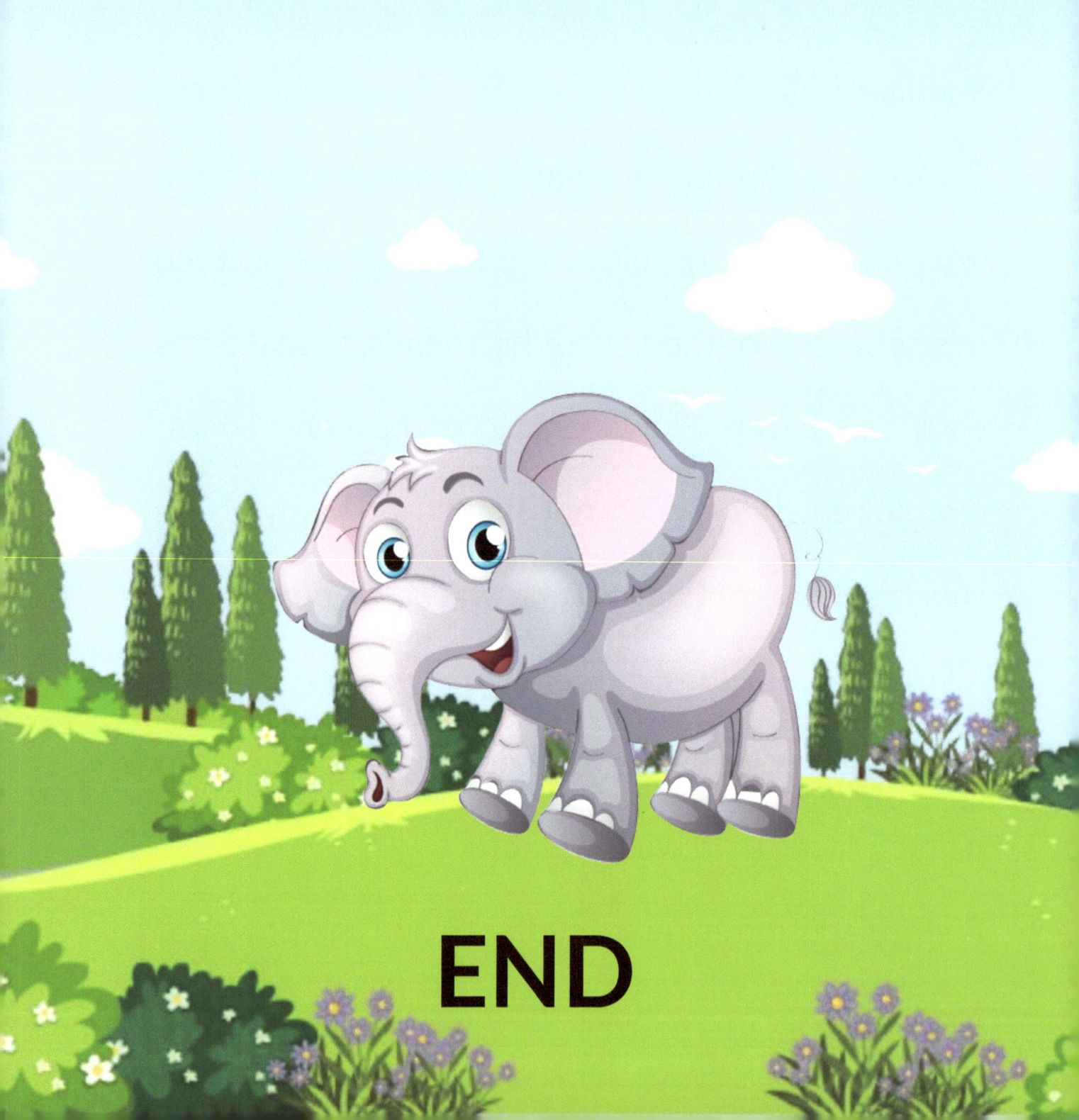

www.ingramcontent.com/pod-product-compliance
Lightning Source LLC
Chambersburg PA
CBHW051835210526
45473CB00005B/1884